COVENTRY AS IT WAS

Virginia Gilbert

On the cover is a reproduction of a drawing of Broadgate by J. S. Austin in 1855. It is interesting to compare it with the fourth photograph, taken from roughly the same viewpoint some 55 years later.

Published by: Hendon Publishing Company Limited, Hendon Mill, Nelson, Lancashire.
Text © Virginia Gilbert 1973

Printed by: Fretwell & Brian Ltd., Howden Hall, Silsden, Keighley, Yorks.

90p

Introduction

With the spread of new building and the demands of steadily increasing road traffic, towns and cities everywhere have altered considerably over the last hundred years, but there is little doubt that Coventry has changed more than most. The wholesale devastation caused by the bombing attacks of World War II and the planning of a new city centre to replace the old, have together removed many landmarks, and in the pages that follow, some attempt has been made to focus attention on those that remain and to look back on scenes that now exist only in the memories of older folk. The illustrations used are all more than fifty years old and form part of the collection belonging to the Coventry and Warwickshire Section of the Reference Library, Coventry. It is believed that copyright in all cases where it did exist has expired, but if oversight in this direction has occurred, apology is extended.

Virginia Gilbert is the Librarian of the Coventry and Warwickshire Section of the Reference Library, Coventry. Born in Leicestershire, she has lived in Kenilworth, another historic place, as long as she can remember, and was educated at Abbotsford School, Kenilworth, Londonderry High School, and later at Loughborough University. She has held various posts in Coventry City Libraries since joining the staff in 1946; she is unmarried and has travelled widely.

An aerial view of Coventry slightly east of the city centre, taken in 1920. The picture is dominated by St. Michael's and Holy Trinity Church, and the long facade of the Council house, then a new building, shows up in the foreground.

The classic view of the three spires, taken from Greyfriars Green about 1885. Sir Thomas White's statue is at the far end of the green.

Broadgate in 1898, looking north to Cross Cheaping. Electric trams were introduced in 1893, and ran until the lines were damaged beyond repair in November 1940.

In contrast, a crowded Broadgate at the proclamation of King George V in 1910. Looking south, the National Westminster Bank now stands on the site of the Coventry Arms and the building next door.

St. Michael's (old Cathedral) aflout 1904. Fortunately, the fine Gothic spire was undamaged by the bombing which destroyed the rest of the building in November 1940, and those who climb the tower are still rewarded with a panoramic view. Note the fields clearly visible within a short distance of the city centre, before the rapid expansion of the twentieth century.

The interior of St. Michael's in the year 1900. Visitors to the open ruins will recognise the tracery of the east window, but may find it hard to visualise the elaborate arcading where now only the bases of the pillars remain. The roof was destroyed by incendiary bombs on the night of 14th November 1940.

Priory Row (in 1890) is one part of central Coventry which has not changed much, except for the glimpse at the far end. The timber framed buildings shown here may have been built soon after the destruction of the Priory church in 1539. They adjoin the ruins of the west end where Earl Leofric and Lady Godiva are believed to be buried.

Holy Trinity Church seen from Priory Row in 1908. Although almost overshadowed by its proximity to the old and new cathedrals, this ancient parish church has a history and charm of its own.

The Benedictine Priory church ruins and the old Bluecoat School building, now used by the Coventry branch of the Samaritans.

TRINITY LANE, COVENTRY.

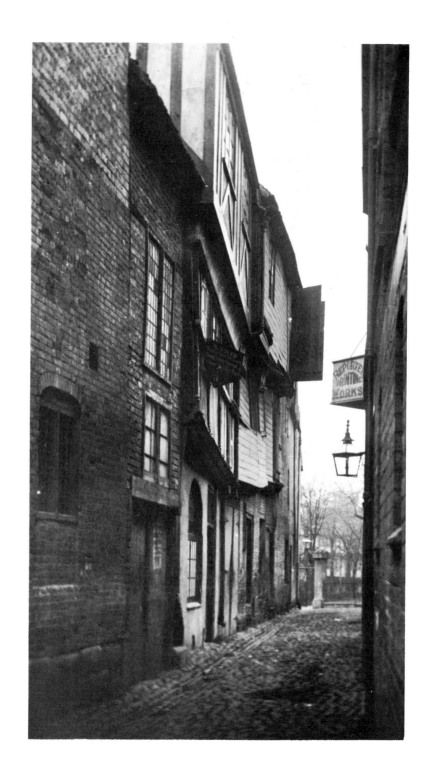

Two narrow lanes in the heart of the city.
Above: Trinity Lane, which once ran between the
churchyard wall and the shops fronting Broadgate.
Right: Derby Lane, which still exists between
Pepper Lane and Holy Trinity. The buildings
either side were mostly destroyed by bombing.

The Gulson Library, built on the site of the old gaol in 1873 and extended in 1890, was destroyed in November 1940 except for the part still in use as the lending library. Nothing remains of the building shown in this picture, but there are plans to replace the present open air cafe with a replica of the Coventry Cross.

The interior of the Reference Library in 1896, now used as the Central Lending Library.

The gateway of St. Mary's Hall in 1866, with Annie Panton as a somewhat overdressed Victorian Lady Godiva, about to take part in the procession which has been held at irregular intervals since 1677-8.

The fourteenth-century Guildhall of St. Mary in Bayley Lane. The cottage in the foreground was once a shop; it is at present a solicitor's office.

The interior of the Great Hall, showing the glories of the north window and the tapestry, which together make a rich medieval setting for the many civic ceremonies held here.

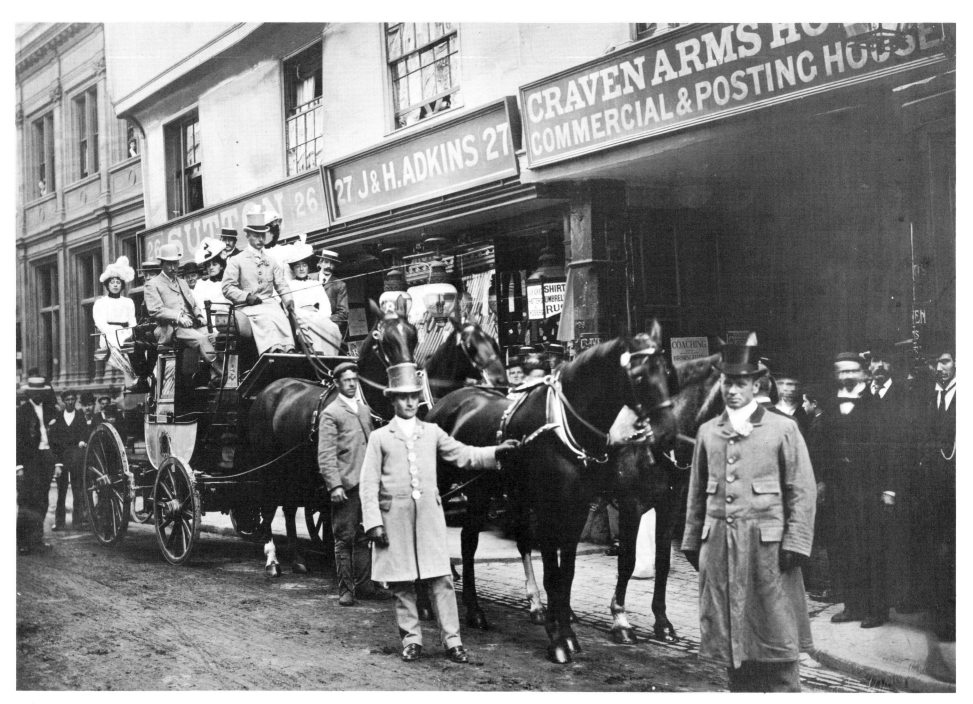

A coach and four outside the old posting house in High Street about 1900, at the end of the coaching era.

The Golden Cross Inn, on the corner of Hay Lane and Bayley Lane. No one knows how long it has stood here, but it is said to be built on the site of an old mint.

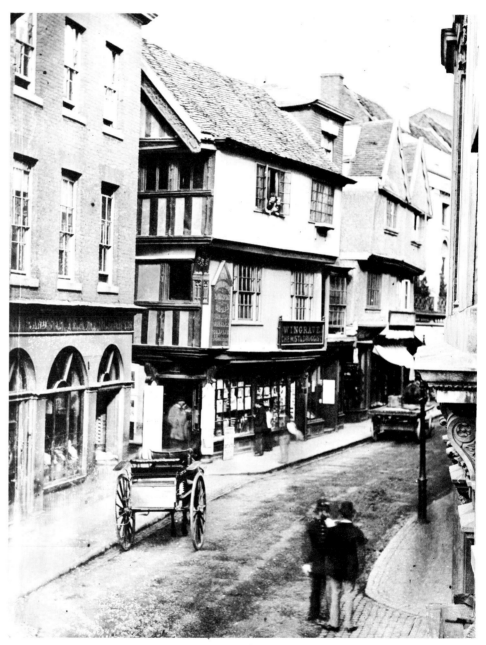

High Street and Pepper Lane corner about 1860. The round-headed windows on the left, now part of a building society office, are the only recognisable feature today.

Palace Yard, a fine old piece of historic Coventry completely destroyed by enemy action in the Second World War. A mixture of architectural styles, it was for many years the home of the Hopkins family, who entertained Royalty here in Stuart times.

The Lady Godiva Procession, Coventry.

Much Park Street in 1907, when the Godiva procession was in progress. Patsy Montagu (La Milo) took the part of the Lady on this occasion.

Whitefriars in the 1890's, when it was in use as a workhouse. The building has had a varied career: first as a Carmelite Priory founded in 1342, then as a private house, and since 1930, it has been used as a Salvation Army Hostel and latterly a museum.

Much alteration and restoration has taken place, but the magnificent cloisters have suffered little.

Ford's Hospital, Greyfriars Lane has been an almshouse since its foundation in 1509. Since 1800 it has been used exclusively for old ladies, each occupying a comfortable room off the little inner courtyard. Looking at it today, the casual observer would not guess that the original building was almost destroyed in an air raid in 1940, when eight of the inmates lost their lives. Skilled reconstruction using some of the salvaged materials has restored its appearance to very much what it was in this photograph of 1900.

The inner courtyard in 1865, with some of the inmates.

The corner of Smithford Street and Broadgate in 1859, showing a top-hatted policeman. Peeping Tom can be seen at the window he occupied before the King's Head Hotel was built.

A close-up of Peeping Tom, the life-size figure which was a well-known Coventry landmark in Smithford Street before the war. He is now in a glass case in the Hotel Leofric coffee lounge.

St. John's Church was originally the collegiate chapel of Bablake, founded by Queen Isabella in 1344. It did not become a parish church until 1734 when it was reported to be in a ruinous condition, and much remodelling and restoration has taken place over the years, but outwardly the fine old sandstone building still looks much as it did in early engravings. This picture was taken about 1910.

Bablake Old School in 1912. This attractive range of black and white buildings complete with cloister forms the eastern side of the quadrangle behind St. John's Church. The school, a survival from the days of the pre-Reformation Gild Chapel, was refounded in 1563 and this building was in use until new premises were opened at Coundon in 1890. Now taken over by the offices of the General Municipal Charities and the school governors, some of the old furnishings and some fine woodwork remain.

Bablake School Band in 1887, showing the quaint long-skirted uniform worn at the time.

Bond's Hospital, (Bablake) in 1900. Possibly Coventry's finest gem of Tudor architecture, this almshouse for old men was founded in 1506 "for so long as the world shall endure". The number of inmates has grown over the centuries, and a great deal of replanning and modernisation has taken place inside, but outwardly the building remains much the same, forming one side of the quiet quadrangle behind St. John's Church.

An old house in Spon End about 1914. Coventry once had a wealth of these medieval timbered dwellings, but the war, the development of the city centre and the inner ring road scheme have removed all but a few.

Spon Street in 1910, looking west. A number of medieval houses in this area have been restored, and others from Much Park Street and Gosford Street have been re-erected here to form a townscape of old Coventry.

Fleet Street in 1900. The buildings behind the railings were demolished to make way for Corporation Street in 1931. Smithford Street in the middle distance is now the Precinct.

The corner of West Orchard in 1909, when the first taxis were displacing hansom cabs.

The old theatre in Smithford Street, built by Sir Skears Rew in 1815. As the Theatre Royal it provided good entertainment until the depression years of the 1860's, after which it became a Music Hall. It finally closed in 1889.

The Market Square in 1910, now the site of the Hotel Leofric.

An early photograph of the first Coventry police station in 1854. The old "lock-up" and stocks stood on the site later occupied by the Market Hall.

Coventry Volunteer Fire Brigade about 1886.

Butcher Row, a picturesque but congested area near the city centre. This picture was taken in 1900 when traffic problems were few, but in 1936 the buildings were removed to make way for Trinity Street.

From early times Coventry Cross stood at the junction of Broadgate and Cross Cheaping, and this one was erected in 1542. An elaborately decorated sandstone pinnacle, it became unsafe and was taken down in 1771.

Cross Cheaping in 1892. This busy thoroughfare leading north from Broadgate to Bishop Street was the site of the medieval market and several historic buildings, such as the Mayor's Parlour.

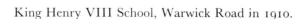

Old Grammar School, Coventry.

The Old Grammar School on the corner of Hales Street and Bishop Street, and one of Coventry's oldest buildings. Originally built as the church of the Hospital of St. John run by the neighbouring Priory for "poor wayfaring men", John Hales acquired the empty building at the Dissolution and opened his Grammar School there. It continued as a school until the present King Henry VIII School buildings were erected in 1885, and is now used as a church hall.

King Henry VIII School, Warwick Road in 1910.

Swanswell or Priory Gate, once the entrance to St.
Mary's Fishponds. It was in use as a shop in 1912,
when this picture was taken.

Cook Street Gate sometime before 1905.

These are the only two remaining gates of the city's twelve, linked by a well preserved section of the town wall which
runs through Lady Herbert's Garden.

Swanswell Pool, Coventry.

Swanswell Pool and the Coventry and Warwickshire Hospital about 1900. The gardens were laid out in 1850, but the pool is shown on the earliest known map of Coventry, dating from 1610. The hospital building was erected in 1864.

Pool Meadow when the Great Fair was held there in 1920. This annual event has been a feature of Coventry life since the Middle Ages and various sites in the city centre were used, until traffic congestion drove it to suburban open spaces. At present it is held on Hearsall Common.

Priory Street Public Baths was the large building shown in the background of the Pool Meadow photograph, and this is a picture of the bathers at the opening ceremony in 1894.

The canal wharf at Foleshill Road at the time of King George V's coronation celebrations in June 1911. Miss Viola Hamilton was Lady Godiva.

The canal at Navigation Bridge in the early years of the century before industrialisation spoiled the surroundings. Once an important commercial link for the coal trade, it is now more used by pleasure boats.

THE COVENTRY FOOTBALL CLUB TEAM.

J. R. Bradshaw.   C. Lea.   A. Rotherham.   A. Slater.   H. D. G. Bennett.   F. Loveitt.   A. Frith.   J. Hadfield.

Mr. A. Bill (Sec.)   C. D. Pole.   R. A. Rotherham.   A. C. Hill (Capt.)   T. A. Cash.   J. Lee.   W. Rice.   Mr. C. Wareham (Touch Judge).

R. H. Graham.   J. J. Richardson.

Coventry Football Club team in 1891, when A. C. Hill was Captain.

A double-decker bus in Walsgrave Road, soon after the service was inaugurated in 1914.

Back to the city centre, and a view of the top of Hertford Street in 1900, showing the King's Head Hotel and the City Hotel on the corners of Smithford Street.

Hertford Street in 1908. Nothing remains of the buildings on the lefthand side, and the whole area is now a traffic-free shopping precinct.

Christchurch about 1910. The spire, 211 feet high and one of Coventry's famous three, has stood since the time of the Greyfriars, but the church in this picture lasted only 110 years. It was built by public subscription in 1830 and destroyed by the bombing in World War II.

Cheylesmore Manor House as it was in 1913. Once the seat of the Earls of Chester, Queen Isabella and her grandson the Black Prince, the manor has played an important part in Coventry's history. Since the war it has been skilfully reconstructed, and is now used as a Registry Office.

The advent of the motor car age—the first Coventry to Birmingham run leaving Greyfriars Green in 1897. Houses in the Quadrant can be seen in the background.

Coventry has had three railway stations since the line was opened in 1838; this is a view of the second one seen from the Eaton Road approach in the early years of this century. The modern building now on the site was erected 1960-2, at the time of the consecration of the new Cathedral.

Warwick Road at the bottom of Station Hill, when it was the scene of a railwaymen's strike in 1911.

The Starley memorial in Queen's Road, erected in 1884, to commemorate James Starley, "the father of the Coventry cycle industry."

The quadruplet "Swift", an example of the cycles manufactured by the Coventry Machinists Company in the 1890's.

A watchmaker's workshop in 1896. J. Masters and Sons of St. John Street had a combined works, office and warehouse typical of the trade.

The interior of J. Player's watchmaking workshop in the Butts, about 1891. In both pictures note the large windows specially designed for maximum daylight, a feature adopted by the weavers in their "topshops".

Coventry houses with George Eliot connections.
Above: Nantglyn, Warwick Row, where she
attended Miss Franklin's school. Right: Bird
Grove, Foleshill Road, her home from 1841 to
1849.